I'm going to big school!

by Beth Thomas

www.transitionstorybooks.co.uk

We might have a story,
then time to play –
I really am very excited!

Last week my teacher came to see me and two other friends at my preschool. I gave her a burger and a carrot in tea, And I told her, "I'm going to big school!"

My teacher was kind and she asked me to say all the things that I like to do. I told her, "sticking and water play,"

My mum made some tea; we had biscuits – yum!
It was nice to just play and chatter.

My teacher asked Mum what I'm like at home –
My Mum said, "mad as a hatter!"

And I've been to my big school already, you know, I went with my mum and her sister.

I made a new friend called Rebecca,
And this week I've really missed her!

But I got mixed up, put my bag on the peg
And my coat with the lunch – what a wally!

She showed us the
loos and the clothes
we will wear;
There really is so much to do!

I walked around and had a good look,
Then I played with a frog that was blue!

So, today I'm going to big school again
And Rebecca will see me there.

We're having a party at preschool next week,

with balloons
and games
and cake!

I'm saying goodbye to lots of my friends —

I don't know how long that will take.

But I know that I will make lots of friends
At big school, like Rebecca, you see.
I'm just so happy to be going to school
and I'm sure my new friends will agree!

Other books by Beth Thomas:

www.transitionstorybooks.co.uk